there now

Also by Eamon Grennan

Poetry

What Light There Is & Other Poems
As If It Matters
So It Goes
Relations: New & Selected Poems
Still Life with Waterfall
The Quick of It
Matter of Fact
Out of Sight: New & Selected Poems

Translation

Leopardi: Selected Poems
Oedipus at Colonus (with Rachel Kitzinger)

Essays

Facing the Music: Irish Poetry in the Twentieth Century

there now

poems

Eamon Grennan

Graywolf Press

This publication is made possible, in part, by the voters of Minnesota through a Minnesota State Arts Board Operating Support grant, thanks to a legislative appropriation from the arts and cultural heritage fund, and through a grant from the Wells Fargo Foundation Minnesota. Significant support has also been provided by Target, the McKnight Foundation, the Amazon Literary Partnership, and other generous contributions from foundations, corporations, and individuals. To these organizations and individuals we offer our heartfelt thanks.

Published in Ireland by the Gallery Press, 2015

Published by Graywolf Press
250 Third Avenue North, Suite 600
Minneapolis, Minnesota 55401

www.graywolfpress.org

Published in the United States of America

ISBN 978-1-55597-754-2

2 4 6 8 9 7 5 3 1
First Graywolf Printing, 2016

Library of Congress Control Number: 2016931140

Cover design: Jeenee Lee Design

Cover art: jaminwell / iStock

For my friends in Renvyle

contents

"An hour
soul-eclipsed. The next, an autumn light."
Paul Celan, "All Souls"

"They had happened into my dimension
The moment I was arriving just there."
Ted Hughes, "Roe-deer"

there now

listen

When the one cow eyeing you with its sniper's spectral gaze
      hears louder than the Angelus bell the big *bó*-bawl
of another cow down near the lake she ups her massy head
      wide-opens a cavernous mouth and bawls back
and for a few huge cow-minutes these two antiphonal plain-chanters
      conduct a world-obliterating duet: a duologue affirming
with each enormous diphthong their earthly unassailable
      real presence—their fully inhabited overflowing moment—
and then it's night and only the small sky-high cry of one
      nightbird over lake-glimmer breaks the silence with its
little lamenting whistle-cry repeating and repeating itself
      into vacancy and the mute eyelessness of space and there's nothing
beyond that naked *nachtmusik* in the dead silent wide-shining fields
      of furze and rushes and bramble bushes of ever-thickening black.

fresh start

Imagine you walk outdoors in a dream
      to discover all the old stone walls
surrounding the cottage garden
      cleared of briars grass hedges—so stones
drawn out of earth and carried and laid down
      to compose an enclosure or a meering fence
are shining as if just now created
      and the whole place figuring a fresh start
with fuchsia leaves and leaves of young ash
      and sycamore and mountain ash
all just now come to life
      and sensing first a stir of air
then suddenly shivering in the near-
      warm arms of the first felt breeze.

oystercatchers in flight

Sea's stony greenblue shatters to white
     in a running swell under noonsky of cloudlight
where on a foamed-over cropping of rock
     a band of oystercatchers faces all one way
into a nor'wester so shafts of windlight
     ignite each orange beak in this abiding
tribe of black till you clap and their risen black
     turns white as they veronica on wind and
then away with them (shrill-pitched as frighted
     plovers only harsher more excited)
and riding the stiff wind like eager lovers straining
     into its every last whim: its pulsing steady
heart-push in every flesh-startling open-eyed
     long-extended deepening sea-breath.

wormwork

When a century of wriggling Lazarites
     slick as slates after rain
that were not dead but sleeping
     in the muck they'd contrived
over three seasons in the pitch-
     dark recesses of timber planks
stacked by the back door
     felt (as you hauled the damp wood
free of wall and wet) the sudden
     riddling scald of light and lethal
heat of it—was it any wonder they
     and the grey tribe of woodlice
(like bewildered villagers dispossessed
     by civil war) headed for grass and
the shelter of hedges or any friendly
     accommodating shade where their
nerves (they being all nerve) could
     settle again in that mulched silence
and resume like instruments of resurrection
     their blind reiterated patient
ever-turning earth-aerating lives?

flower

I'm thinking of those North African flowers
        called *Belles de Nuit*: moonlight-loving
rouge-magenta blooms the book says
        are plants of sadness (*Herbes Tristes*)
and elsewhere *Four O'Clock* or *Marvels*
        of Peru: mouth-open harvesters
of scents till dawn and then deep sleepers
        in their richly petalled beds of shut-light
all day long invisible among their
        leaves dusk-coloured . . . pretending
to be not there at all yet each concocting
        inside its own night-luminescence
simples to settle ills and cool fevers.

body

What I'm hearing is the tramp all trochees of your heart
       inside my head when I lie across your warm breast
to comfort you this morning after a night of ills that kept us
       awake and aware of the body and its cares—
and caring for it.

spring connections

Leafgreen scurf of pollen on the meadow pond
       blizzard of bridal-white blossom in breeze-gust
two redtails idling high on a thermal and higher
       in widening circles till they must be near
out of each other's sight but not sound as one lets out
       a cutting screech that scars spring-blue air and
the other in a long jagged sickle-tooth screech calls back.

little winterscape

Stopping to contemplate the colours
      of the logs you're stacking . . .
you breathe in their creams and pale russets
      chocolate knotholes and slivers of sable
all shining in this light while the cold air
      readies for snow and your own breath
stains it when you take a breath
      to take things in: a kingfisher's *hakkakkak*
or the worn out frost-knobbled ground
      or how those juncos (foul-weather friends)
rise tinkling in a white-tipped spray
      of brown wings or the sight over there
where in emaciated sunshine two girls sit
      to picnic on a patch of dead grass
and when one peels the gleam from a
      clementine to hand a segment over
how the flush of the fruit centres
      the scene and how their paired faces glow.

flesh

These gooseberries of Adriaen Coorte start out of the dark
        to make a small world of in-lit gleaming spheres
whose red is the very colour Mars might be if glimpsed
        in a dream—but translucent too with bittersweet radiance
that is perhaps of the flesh itself found once in quietude
        and not to be denied no matter what happens
for it is beyond question "a grace afforded after all."

It could be a painting: cascades
      of all-night rain have washed it
so all is this blazing early morning
      a starting over—awake to its
reds blues greens its furious rainbows
      and there's no stopping
the kinetic flow of its rekindled dazzle
      as colours run riot and hover
between glossy photograph and abstraction's
      visionary blur—for the downpour
has inflamed the grass and brought out
      birds to flaunt their colours
where they splash in puddles
      so a luminous glow gilds everything
and on the darkened bark
      of the beech tree near the Observatory
splatters of lichen (bean-green star-coins
      in a firmament of muddy grey)
are blazing.

word

There's a word you've met but once and now forgotten
     for the spoon-shaped concave under your Adam's apple:
a small pouch that must be kissed and kissed again
     by lovers learning the ins and outs of one another
and where last night in the sleeping dark a lone mosquito
     inserted itself and drew fresh blood and left
venom and a couple of love-bites
     then left without waking you although this morning
you'll blaze with the minute but unassuageable
     pain of them—which only that word that's vanished
into the mud of memory might be the right cooling balm for.

silence

Nothing to say standing heartsick at the gaping
      light-broached mouth of the stone shed
where last night the black-as-midnight mink
      sucked the life out of all your neighbour's
yellow-eyed hens and out of the four white
      green-smeared eggs in the nest in which
new life had begun to pulse—so you stand there
      in stone silence under the unwavering gaze
of the standing stones on the *tulach* of Tully
      that have held their peace and kept their counsel
for millennia in silence uncompromised while grass
      rustled and night after night the mountain sheep
cried out and wind went on slapping at lakewater
      hiss-whispering its wordless dirge to the reeds
beating time to the near-silent steady footsteps
      of whatever predator might be seeking
any small heart alive to any rustle in the unending
      wrestle between *Bring on more life!*
and that remorseless hunger that would end it.

sculpted

Giacometti

Not *Horseman, Pass By!* but *L'homme qui marche*
      is the truth to be found in his startled geometry
of jagged bronze bones about to leave
      the space they've been spancelled to—as if
one archaic standing boy had heard a call
      that aged him all of a sudden and sent him
stepping through the centuries with a gleam of purpose
      till he finds himself mid-stream among our
crowded lanes and boulevards on fire with questions.

Serra

When that monumental lightness loomed over me
      like the prow and bow of a great liner
a curve of such purity that its weight was
      lifted and it gave itself
to the jeweled rust-red in the butterfly's wing—
      I stopped for a silent minute inside its labyrinth
of weathered steel to wonder whether all
      would be in butterfly time
revealed illuminated understood.

trees abiding

Battered though they've been by fire rain incessant wind
       our ash and sycamore still put out green shoots and leaves
that whisper in any passing breeze and offer perch
       and resting post to blackbird goldcrest wren
that flash and shadow-dash among them and wait
       for Brother Bread to scatter morning manna on gravel
while they clutch these trunks scarred by circumstance
       which they know only as the state and nature
of the world they pass through as it passes through them
       with nothing more (or less) than the usual swerve
from catastrophe to appetite and back—and so they flutter
       down and feed when they need and risk each moment
for the moment: quick in the lichen-lit twisted limbs
       half-ravaged but still upright still abiding
of these trees.

listening to renoir

"Eat" cries his *Village Street* "this paint!"
        or sip his thirsty blues in *The Seine*
at Chatou or inhale those airy clouds
        in *The Gust of Wind* from 1872
when he kept saying "life passes
        have a stab at it": at these white sails
never the same again or at these tiny
        figures in the tall grass who've just been
harvesting mussels or this black gondola
        or these waves just daubs of white
with *soupcons* of violet . . . and now note
        The Woman in the Boat and the tall thin
girl-boy nuzzling one chalk-chested cat
        and that seaweed-green wine carafe
The Woman from Algiers keeps her dark
        come-hither eyes off and how
could you fail to note the unignorable
        unforgettable breasts of *La Baigneuse*
au Griffon . . . and bless before you go back
        to the world he's brought home to you
in all its spectral plenitude
        his own true eyes sure hand.

truffles

Why the word "truffles" in the mouth brings to light and life
        some deep sense of earth in all its unbidden riches
and the quickened way we plunge among them (every sense
        awake and alert for smelling tasting touching whatever
they offer as steam ascends from the hot coil of olive oil
        and pasta while the truffle knob is waiting to be grated
over it)—is because so *here* in this moment we truly *are*:
        hungry-eyed all appetite and saying the good word.

locust tree vision

Where the branches of the honey locust
      thronged through daylight hours
with the wings and voices of bluejays
      finches cardinals chickadees and white-
throated sparrows . . . all making their
      spring-loaded hunger-honed presence
clearly known—now near midnight
      under a clouded sky a solitary
raccoon's plump shape with swingeing tail
      is a solid squat shadow aloft
on a bare bough—a dark body sunk
      it seems in monkish meditation
or an almost otherworldly visitor
      in stillness keeping its own counsel
and receiving through every
      ready hair and wiry nerve
and along each pulsing vein
      and into every quiver of
each electric cell and open pore
      our shared earth's vibrations.

at the fish market

Is it the flamboyant array of gingko leaves
      yellowing along Ninth Street
or the fillets of brazen Brazilian Pintero
      whose scales fashion a repeat-with-variations
ideogram (jet-black and silver)
      for God knows what . . . or is it
the fishmonger sliding his honed blade neat
      between the bones and dense white flesh
of the headless big fish he's filleting
      on his speckled marble or is it the milky
green to emerald avocado of these sweet
      New Zealand cockles come a long way
to find their blind date with destiny
      that has him wondering what it might be like
not to have been as he chose to be
      in the years of hap and hope:
always at odds with the choppy sea
      of happenstance he swam in—
imagining what safe passage?

know your place

Resident alien in this familiar space
    where the smell of wet mud or sight
of the honeycomb shard of a wasp's
    broken home or the slippery
underfoot feel of clover in hummocking clusters
    or a soft rain-sound striking what's left
of the leaves of maple or beech or dogwood
    all conspire to keep you close
although here is no anchoring truth
    to entrust what you used to call
faith to . . . though still (rootless not roofless)
    you can still dibble in the patch
you've been granted by the way things are:
    still bury your hands in it
to coax something up from its under-earth
    of possibility: birdskull or pebble
of pink quartz or one turquoise shard
    of antique glass or even the smell
of dead leaves or a lingering trace of
    kitchen herbs—their fugitive fragrances.

manet's firing squad

Beyond the caverns of city shadow these blindfolded men
      marked with white paper hearts over beating hearts must wait
flexing their toes in brown mudboots till the painter puts the final
      finishing touch to Maximilian whose hand may rest at last
in the milkwhite hand of melancholy Carlota and whose bootblack
      beard has not yet tangled in the smoke that stains the scarlet
flash from the muzzle almost tipping his candid breast—bringing
      everything to be grasped in this crowded little spacetime
to a full stop.

middle east marketplace

But no sign now of its flowers or birds
　　　　its waters cool rooms gardens
nor all the haggle-voices flaring
　　　　from that flagrant bazaar of scarves
spices and pomegranates
　　　　or over the blood-sprinkled
iridescent gleamings of the fish stall:
　　　　all lost to the ring of faces leaning
over the body of one of their own
　　　　splayed naked and face down
at path-edge . . . where some of the
　　　　stopped onlookers hold cell-phones
high for a better picture of the wire-
　　　　bound wrists and close-cropped hair:
the sweat staining that khaki shirt . . .
　　　　those stark muscular buttocks.

fullness

"Overflowing with life" says Socrates in Valéry
      which could be said too of my old neighbour
who stands on his own worn threshold to show me
      how the newspapers have piled up unread since March
while one rusted bucket and a rusty wheelbarrow go on
      shaping a still life on grass cattle-cropped and
"green to the very door" . . . and could be said too of his
      brindle-cow in calf whose carried creature I can see
soft-pulsing in tune and time to its mother's entranced
      and steadily ruminative chewing.

moon doings (renvyle)

Through flawlessly pewtered air this moonlight night
     casts soft-edge shadows while the lake's a moon-scoured
stainless steel and overhead the Dipper etches in starpoint
     its enormous implement and grass grows a shade of grey
recalling what daylight does to operatic cloudbanks
     while across open fields brimming with silver-smitten
shapes of thornbushes and sycamore leaves and spiny
     stilled rushes a single swan-white cottage glows.

morning light

It's on the flat ladder of light
       the cat refuses to come in on
that morning happens this morning
       with small birdshadows printing
images fleet as their flight on it—
       and it's because you hear mouth-
music of morning as mourning music
       that you can do little this minute
but look where the sycamore leaves
       are doing the jig called *Ticklewind*
while infant leaves of the holly tree
       glisten in stiff-pointed speckle-green
bronze . . . as if quick-cast by Rodin
       after *Thought* and before *Kisses*.

tempest

"Uscir di pena / È diletto fra noi"
Leopardi, "La quiete dopo la tempesta"

It's the way stormclouds translate air to a mash
of squirrel grey and something like lightlessness
while dust's a sudden swirl of brown-twister mini-images
of the god Tornuda at his wind-work
and it's the way my students shelter and look out and up
while some run between buildings and all are silenced
by what's about to happen . . . and then in the aftermath
when downpour has dwindled to a trickling and some
shreds of blue appear and light comes back
it's the way they drift from all corners like survivors
soaked to the skin and glittering and laughing
that reminds me how Leopardi knew one afternoon
in Recanati the storm blown over and the happy chatter
of birds and (ordinary as ever) good life coming back.

lively

In Gauguin's *Nature Mort with Cats*
     everything is equally alive: the lilies
freesias jonquils and something blue
     with an orange spot dead centre
plus a dark urn-shaped vase of
     yellow splotches: all (in their chalky
spheres of light) vivid and living
     and ready to spring off the canvas
as are his two cats striped and white-
     chested: one cupped in its own circle
of doze while the other's a wide-awake
     triangle face all furrowed brow and
arrowed ears pink nose and (deep-
     set in that assassin head) two remote
hard-staring aster-blue eyes.

winter city food market

Croakers snappers silver trout striped bass
      ubricone cranberry Stilton and all forms of meat
on and off the bone . . . plus the pout of one
      catwalk wanna-be who's checking her own
thereness in the glass wall that is the market's window—
      make up the city as is and as this homeless
huddle of rags (astride a steam vent on the corner
      to keep body-soul together and get from
hapless today to tomorrow) hopelessly knows it.

colour scheme

Fallen needles of white pine turn the colour of paprika
          now Hudson Valley orchards are rubied with unpicked apples
while at the centre of Route 87 a fallen wild turkey shows off
          his metal-green and ebony feathers blown about
by the blind slipstream of traffic while his broad-taloned feet
          are a clean surprise in black and silver with their toes
still pointing and all a most lamentable flitter and hapless flutter
          of plumage . . . and this is what any journey offers
the quick in passing: there the dead in their unrepeatable colours
          and here the amber candle of a Fall birch to light your way
towards some unknown city (*how did you get here? is this*
          a dream?) where you'll take a ruminative saunter
among the shop- and office-windows and see to your surprise
          the black shadow of your own reflected stranger-face
in there: that odd body adrift and all at sea among strangers.

survivor (new orleans 2007)

Hard to believe the green patch this egret shelters her yellow feet in
        while glowing in the shade spread by surviving live oaks
was only a little while back a brackish flood taking the city by surprise
        and leaving it desolate and leaving behind this bird
patient in her proper perch on dry grass and that at my approach
        opens the white light of her wings and tucks her coal-black
spindle legs and (being like her kind a survivor whose every bone
        knows the art of keeping going) slow-rises on the now mild air
and goes.

one winter sunday on long beach island

Beside slabs of frozen sand like polished hip bones
      and tawny-amber eggshell-brittle crab claws
and green seaweed coating break-rocks
      that shine like translucent quartz
and big gulls unfolding their glittery
      gridwork of wings in early light
while one of them cries out in its own forlorn
      bi-dialect of sand and sea
at the waves re-grinding shards of sea-glass
      to a pale emerald gleam . . .
I can see in hard sunshine
      under sounds of surf churning dark water
beat by beat to light
      how a few butterflies are making
steady progress south
      along the eastern sand-line
and hovering above the green hummocks
      of endangered dunes and stopping
to sip at the barely nodding yellow lips
      of some late-blooming goldenrod
which monarchs lemonyellows and lilywhites
      spend sweet sabbatical down-time
feeding on.

dead redtail

Since under that wing-canopy spanning field after field
      our world was laid out once for her highbright
death-dealing eye to pasture on—who would ever have
      thought she could lie in such a small huddle as
these shattered wings make with their feathers all
      matted from the wan-grey hawk-maculating mud
and pale machine-made dust of the persistently sifted
      oil-stained diesel-scented earth of the Jersey Turnpike?

storm and star

"So quick bright things come to confusion."
A Midsummer Night's Dream

In the grip of mania today's weather is turn
        and turn about: rain to shine sun to shade
so one minute you're wet to the skin the next
        blown almost to kingdom come and gone
by a wind that tosses bog-grass about and ragged
        sheep-fleece . . . while rain blinds you and
the gale deafens and binds like the vice-grip
        of any forbidden dreamshape—the ache
of its unbreakable fever searing you in sleep
        so you risk a sheer disappearing with nothing
left of you but smoke: a rose-shot grey
        on bitumen grey and fingered into the quicksilver
quaint mnemonic figure (clearly limned
        but quick-shooting from sight across the vast
heart-scalding dark) of last night's single
        disappearing star.

bonnard's eyes

He says it's by the seduction of the *first idea*
        the painter may attain to the *universal*
and today (pondering the Taoist *Virtue of*
        Useless Wandering) you may catch
a glimpse of it in those cottony yellow wisps
        that say *wych hazel* or in the rust-red breast
of one foraging robin or in the feel of ground
        giving ground under winter boots or in
the way bird-voices orchestrate air as
        cardinals robins red-winged blackbirds
nuthatches and three kinds of woodpecker
        stake their claims to space where each
will make its home . . . and perhaps in these
        first ideas you too may find that *universal*
the painter glimpsed in the ever-glow of his
        wife's body as she drew it under or
out of water so the whole array of flowers
        ointments mirrors mats and straw-baskets
grew radiant and his eyes (lost in their
        own *useless wandering*) found a rooted
home to come home to.

sand martins departing

"It lives in winding holes in sheer sandy hills."
    Linnaeus

On the eastern side of this sandy sea-cliff
    (for September morning warmth and in the lea
of prevailing westerlies) a family of sand martins
    fills salt air with their shrill chatter—swooping
on stretchwings over where a wide swath
    of their pueblo has fallen and left just
a handful of nests like small sockets of darkness
    where they cling with shivering wing and
quickened shriek then vanish into the mystery
    their silence leaves in its wake as they slip
through chambering vacancies in the cliff-face
    and catch their breath and ready their collective
heart for the long autumn haul that will toss them
    all twitter-talk on auspicious gales south then
south again to winter.

gone

The little house grows quiet now she's gone from it
      and so he'll set small orange embers of montbretia in a vase
before the bedroom mirror although its petals can behold
      no more than themselves in the cold truth-telling glass.

window world

Through your vigilant window you see
      a lace of misty rain drawn across Letter Hill
by a sou'wester and how in the near field
      the bull gently nudges his favorite
among the herd so she rises to her knees
      then stands in all her silky sheen
and they move off nonchalantly together
      and you imagine waking from
a fretful dreamscape into this play of light
      over the garden empty of everything
except the long intake and let-out of
      windbreath among ash and sally leaves . . .
with shaft after shaft of green light
      breaking in silence across the grass
as you leave one otherworld for another
      in the here and now in which your
rain-laced window sets its pitiless sights
      on what simply is and you adjust to it.

while

While history happens and the garden's gravel path
      becomes grass again what he feels is the blunt tongue
coming up against the edgy flicker and untranslatable quick
      of what looks him full in the face while
bushes push disheveled branches up into light
      and the burgeoning grass takes over every inch
and the colonizing weeds with pink or purple or yellow heads
      shape constellations while the birds in their quotidian
busyness glimmer in and out of shadow under the everlasting
      bulk of Tully Mountain and above the platinum blue
pulsations of the lake while the ever-changing light is up
      again as always to its old unspeakable unstoppable tricks.

rats

Scratch-scurry of rat-nails overhead
      where they scamper across attic boards
and with desperate teeth drag at the poison
      laid for these disturbers of the peace
of sleep—these low-bellied squeak-
      squatters of darkest corners
that have crept out of the weather
      to cross-hatch themselves
into your dreams
      and be an agitation of the nerves
as if what's unspeakable were made flesh
      and all your deep-buried distresses
resurrected and released into the light of day
      to dare you again (against the grain
and flinch as you might)
      to find words for them . . . though you feel
no pity for the death that has to happen:
      only antique horror at having the space
above your head invaded by creatures
      of such sharp dark-fixed intent
triggered by nothing but bright teeth
      and ravening appetite
to eat you out of house and home
      by gnawing to the bone
each tingling terrified toothsome morsel.

october reward

No doubt the gunmetal grackles are stirring
      among the sturdy stems of goldenrod
but what I notice after a slow morning simmer
      has turned everything its Midas-light touches
into an aspect of dazzle is the single lemon-yellow
      butterfly small as a postage stamp
and flying sideways in zigs and zags until it
      finds almost buried in grass the one
remaining still-untouched dandelion and lights
      and settles into it with its fragile breeze-blown
near-infinite persistence this once rewarded.

dayrise to darkfall

Wren rising from wet grass to vanish
  little troglodyte among stones of the wall
cows gone from the near field and their
  daily mushing the rushes to muck
blockish Duchruach in its morning cloud
  of haze hemming it with slate-shade . . .
and morning to noon the garden jumpy
  with bird-noise—its mild or agitated
arias of warning or love or hunger or
  something we've no name for . . .
but what's to be said at all for the guillemot
  that ran foul last night of the light
over the Inn door and was found
  flapping like mad among bottles
and discarded boxes until coaxed into
  the safe swaddle of a dishtowel and
left out of harm's way in the mud-churned
  field across the road and leaving us
to wonder could it smell the sea
  and get there before the fox found it.

by moonlight

She's *interested* (if that's the word) in you—this young deer
      among leafless trees behind the house and the two of you
stock-still after midnight in moonlight that's a gleam in the dark
      pool of her eye that takes you in as a solid tall shadow
to her way of *thinking* (if that's the word) until as you inch closer
      she *huffs* then raises the white flag of her tail and takes
one bound over rackety branches into a deep invisibility you keep
      peering into while the keen half-moon beams down
on your lone left shade that casts no shadow: just another
      breathing creature in a nightworld brimming with collisions.

fog

"O curlew, cry no more . . ."
                    Yeats, "He Reproves the Curlew"

Since the curlew has chosen to cry some more
            (if only over the clouded slopes of Letter Hill)
and since the small haycocks in the near field stand
            like sack-clothed Japanese sages contemplating
two quartz-white Connemara mares that contemplate
            them back in sea-deep silence—and since pines
and oak trees ring my neighbor's house like meditative elders
            of some remote silent order considering what
counsel they might offer . . . perhaps it's time to take
            thought for the journey along the strait road
though with wave after wave of wet fog now rolling
            off the Atlantic I can barely see beyond the red
and green borders of the garden whose fuchsia leaves
            and grass blades shiver a little with chill when
mist hits them while small birds lose their coordinates
            (no lake no mountain) and cluster round the feeder
in frantic chatter . . . since in their consciousness
            things are simply happening and again happening
in a livid blank and this foggy drizzle-day is simply
            there beyond question and the mist not lifting.

eyes not at rest

Upriver you see water wide-spread again its opalescent hands
      while cloud-shadows collage patterns and the world strobes
over your eyes until one split-second knife-edge dart of light
      lets you see the black sequin on the finch's beak as the bird
pries from the pendant feeder's wire mesh the sweet
      heart of a sunflower seed and is gone in a flash . . .
so you find yourself looking with heightened attention again
      at the abandoned feeder that makes with its distinct small
pendulum-swings against the window this persistent ticking sound.

no end to it

Not even the slow rain falling
      on the crowded roundabout in Castlebar
is as sad as the sound of her crying
      miles away with the sad Atlantic
setting itself between them
      and his voice unable to take the weight
off her heart so when she falls silent
      he hears only his own silence—thick
as an ocean icing over or complete
      as the quiet of that badger that lies
clean as a cat's tongue and stone dead
      with its nose in the dust of the road
from Currywongaun to Kylemore
      and knows no more what came down
on its shortsighted life than the leaf
      knows twisted off the sycamore
and starting to be side-road dust
      in such a silence as you imagine
the moon might sequester on night
      after empty night of bare-bone
rock-strewn bitter chill and no end to it.

with rainbow and two ravens

Whatever that rainbow might mean those ravens never mind it
        as they spindrift over High Road houses calling to each other
with such lofty indifference for anything that might otherwise
        distract them from their coupled delight in tumble and spin
with jet wings spread or tucked so they sudden-spiral earthwards then
        opening fanning rising into such breath-taking long glides
they have to shout for the sheer joy of it . . . or so I imagine—
        keeping sky-watch through binoculars from my own plot
(grounded below their high jinks) and plotting (one eye fixed on
        that fading rainbow) the ever-shifting distance between them.

what's there

"This" says Li Po (ending a poem
      in praise of the dark green mountain)
"is a different world not of the human kind . . ."
      and I might say the same
seeing how morning light falls on Letter Hill
      in shapely swaths of green and brown
so the heather and bracken fashion some
      greater sense than language can manage . . .
the way those yesterday shapes of light
      and shade on the laneway near Kylemore
let me in for a speechless minute
      to a sense of something simply *beyond*—
though when I emerged again
      with all my wits onto the main road
it was just as simply gone: as gone
      as that moment when on his way
up-country into the interior Bashō observed
      "under a pine tree a smattering
of people who'd renounced this world
      quietly living in a grass hut
from which smoke rose from a fire
      of gleanings and pine cones" . . .
or as gone as the night when
      lying by an inn's open window
he "lay in the midst of rain and cloud"
and remembered the moon shining on the sea
      and felt "mysteriously exhilarated."

sudden dark

in memoriam, S.H.

Although I couldn't shoulder his coffin like those
       who carried him out of the ordinary into the marvellous
I still have to take the pressing heft and ponder of it to heart
       and feel the grave weight of the great absence he'd become
by leaving us that way in his wake to make the best of it
       with the whole place emptied out and the left bereft
rest of us seeking about among what remained of him
       for the right way to say sorry say grief say the silence
and find in it (as he would) some smallest shard of light—
       pointed and painful to touch but still a glimmer
to inch us step by wary step out of the sudden dark
       we find ourselves at a loss in and no such other help coming.

among the elements in a time of war

Fog's white tongue says nothing
     licking mountain and field and lake
so they're struck dumb to nothing
     in their base dialects of airy light
though last night's heavens were alive
     with stars all chanting their canticle
of fire . . . and now you see how water
     in this glass jug will not stop trembling—
as if its agitation were some secret
     worry the solid earth under our own
uneasy feet feels at each meniscus-shiver
     as surface ruptures a little and ordinary
objects of the world stutter
     as if the stricken face of earth itself
with its indifference for a moment broken
     could not stop sobbing.

crumbs

No question crumbs aren't everything
      but when small birds fuss among them
squabbling for a shiny morsel
      with their coloured feathers snagging light
and their tiny eyes on fire with the focused
      fury of their hunger . . . then the brute fact
of what birds are up against
      has to be acknowledged: that this
December wind chills beyond
      feather-protection . . . that famine happens.

the cézanne minute

It's how birds are awake to that single minute
      in the life of the world that keeps going by
that keeps you keeping a peeled eye on them
      in their infinitely minute changes of colour
as each speedy heartbeat hammers its own brisk
      rivet of breath onto air you're staring through
at them while "Breathe in now" says Cézanne
      as he eyeballs another brilliant square inch
of the perpetually unsettling here and now
      gone world "and hold it."

early morning jog

And the geese the kingfisher the dove the dead chipmunk
      and the one tree turned the saffron of a monk's *sanghati*
and the mist scarfed between high pine branches and the big-
      boughed London plane tree and the single pink almost
full-blown rose and the shrill choir of starlings rounding the chapel
      belfry and the sleek dew-dabbled gleam highlighting three
blue bikes that have leaned all night against the knobbled barks
      of pine and maple and walnut and here's the night shift
starting sleepy-eyed for home and there's the grey-rimmed halo
      risen round the squirrel's tail and now the sudden illumination
of roof-slates and now your sweat your breath your aching knees.

memento

Scattered through ragtaggle underbrush
      starting to show green shoots
lie the dark remains of rail-sleepers
      napping now beside the rusted-out
wreck of a Chevy that was once sky-blue
      and is nothing now but shattered panels
and anonymous engine scraps
      in the ditch by a path that was a railway line
cut once between small hills whose silence
      has not been broken for fifty years
by the rattle and lonesome-blown
      whistle of a train and whose air
hasn't carried for ages the smell
      I'd catch as a sandboy (near
Seapoint on the coastal line)
      of coal smoke and hot steam . . . all
puffed up in great white cloud-breaths
      out of that once-upon-a-time
storybook black-sooted chimney.

world word

What over the gable-end and high up under tangled cloud
       that raven might be saying to its tumble-soaring mate
or what the blackbird might intend when chattering among
       scattered breadcrumbs or what the bellowing of one cow
then another in the near field might mean remains beyond
       my ken—being all noise for which no words will manage
though all is language settling and unsettling the world
       beyond me . . . and yet there's the dunnock in all its
dun colours at work among the small stones and patchy grass
       of the driveway and here's the robin's aggressive tilt
at breadcrumbs and there goes the sudden shriek
       of the blackbird . . . all alive inside the inhuman
breath-pattern of the wind trawling every last leaf
       and blade of grass and flinging rain like velvet pebbles
onto the skylight: nothing but parables in every bristling inch
       of the out-of-sight unspoken never-to-be-known pure
sense-startling untranslatable *there* of the world as we find it.

paint

Amazing how it's only paint that does it:
        matching mud ruts in a pitted lane for Hobbema
or a pool of waterlight among tree shadows
        for Ruisdael or a drunkard's nose for a face
fixed up by Rembrandt to tell us nothing
        except how poor flesh falls in on itself . . .
and still you haven't mentioned those still lifes in
        odd corners with their many-angled vessels
and all those loaves of bread and sides of
        beef and the bowls the pumpkins or those
translucent lemon gems plumped with tartness
        or those sober goblets of cheap glass or fine
crystal with the live wine still winking in them.

dreamscape with clouds and seagirl

"Swimming light, will you come now?"
Celan, "With Letter and Clock"

Is it possible to tranquilize with this jewelled sunset
          past sundown (sky in its immaculate mix
of peach and gold . . . its great Gaudi-gaudy edifices
          erecting themselves in cloud
to build the City of Nowhere on the horizon . . .
          and the islands only shapes of whale
or turf reek or flattened sphere on a sea
          so still it might be walked on)—
possible to tranquilize with all this
          the heart-stunning dream of evening's turbulence
with its seagirl emerging from waves in her
          wet gleam-enveloped flesh and grave face
all alight beside him and her sudden upturned
          forward yielding unexpected kiss?

with birds and one dead leaf

On the one hand these snow flitters
        are a flurry of sun-splintering
frozen air while on the other
        a flock of cedar waxwings
makes a hungry high-pitched cheeping
        in its winging from one
hope-laden fruit tree to another
        and then there's a carnival
of crested birds at the feeder: cardinals
        carved blood-red with their
orange-lipstick ladies and the downy
        woodpecker zebra-streaked
and the toothpick legs of the chickadees
        and the polished crimson topknot
of a red-bellied woodpecker and
        juncos and sparrows and one nuthatch . . .
all making a crazy cracked music:
        an extravaganza almost phantasmagoric
that only amplifies (when night falls
        and the garden falls silent at last)
the desiccated skitter of one fleet
        dead leaf scuttling swift as
any fieldmouse over hardened snow.

things in the vicinity

"Small world! / You could almost hug it!"
Wislawa Szymborska, "Séance"

It's the lightning wings of chaffinches
      where they squabble over breadcrumbs
or it's dew droplets flashing on grassblades
      or simply it's the fact that one minute
in the life of the world this autumn morning
      is as Cézanne says *going by! paint it as is!*
that makes me bend again to the page
      my live and accidental hand is shadowing.

to sit

He wonders what the manic squawk of a laughing gull could make
        of the momentum of a life that sits and practices knowing itself
under the mild eye of May sunshine and in the scented arms
        of an easterly breeze off the almost still sea and how there's nothing
to be done as the pointed grasses nod and the dunes start to show
        a few yellow flowers and any hour now a white or amber butterfly
will waver over dunegrass to sip at whatever nectar cocktail
        the season's concocted out of its flowery butterfly-inviting store
whose fullness will for the moment be as it's always been enough.

leaving

Emplaned and cutting all connections you move at speed
　　　　through wet greens of Shannon and up into the blank
stage-curtain of mist to a blind nothing that grows lighter
　　　　every second until blue happens and then that's it:
the whole island a vanished thing where yesterday
　　　　you saw and heard a flock of airborne mourners (curlews
and plovers) winging into their own vanishing
　　　　while the wind (a steady slapping at your shoulders)
whipped the sea to a rock-dousing cosmos of foam from which
　　　　one tern two gulls three shrieking oystercatchers
twist away as tempest takes them as air now takes you
　　　　into the blue with the sun behind you the way
yesterday you caught it catching one jackdaw on a fencepost
　　　　and polishing him to a deep sheen that turned him
for a minute of stillness into an ebony icon of the place
　　　　you were leaving—before the bird (remembering birdness)
opened his wings and slowly rose and stayed spread-winged
　　　　for a moment and only then shook off the place he'd been
and drifted first then flapped hastily away the way you've
　　　　had to: having bolted doors and windows and left
the families of chaffinches quarrelling among the crumbs
　　　　and the cat licking last milk off its whiskers
while the bees keep trawling and testing the fuchsia—
　　　　as it shall be forever (if we let them) for nectar.

reminder

So here is *oblique light* splintering along an iced puddle
  and here two red-tails standing tall totem-like
and cream-chested at the bald top of a white pine
  and there the fallen leaves of a beech inscribing
a circle of rust and gold and here comes Heraclitus
  having his own say about just about everything:
to recall with no rejoinder possible that the fairest
  order in the world is a heap (*Better believe it!*)
of random sweepings.

owl light

Standing vigil on sea-verge at Letterfrack inlet
  the heron's a pale mist-grey and faint translucence
among ambers and blacks of sea-wrack while
  plovers bescreech the rainswept tide by Glassilaun
where a family of terns hovers before plunging as
  white projectiles into the indigo and avocado water
and the young cry out as they learn to dive for
  their lives and carry their tribe into a future
of fish and ecstasy while wind-driven spongy
  rain-rags are shawling Letter Hill where
a drenched cow is bellowing and then it's evening
  and Venus is a small sphere of silver simmering
in the west under clouds daubed ochre peach
  and slate-grey and then the little things kick in
with child-bleatings of bare sheep on the mountainside
  whose dirt-shredded shearings are left to languish
in barns beside which the brown flicker of a chaffinch
  can be seen between ash branches while
all the while Dürer's owl looks down on the man
  at his writing table and "Here" (says the owl)
"one way or another by clockface or starlight . . . here we are."

anemones beheld by rachel

How not look again at these vased anemones whose thirsty stems
       drink up water for their ceremony of reds purples pinks . . .
all dying for light oozing through our dining-room window and all
       (*look you!*) living for the moment in it and for the moment
after that as if on fire?

different mergansers

Red beak white breast and head of sooty black:
> this *Common Merganser* is a study in *rouge et noir*
at ease on inland water where (henna-crested)
> his lustrous mate will answer with eager eye
his every light-quickened glance—their migrant
> intermission of peace a far cry from that wave-
wilderness their cousin the *Red-breasted Merganser*
> stretches his urgent solitary wings in and (native
of solitude) looks about all patience—all alone as he is
> and all unlike this one that lifts *rouge* beak
noir head and glances back uxorious at his mate
> taking it easy in the sun of their spring migration
and tossing her henna-red tousled head as if to say
> there's no such crest as his (full-fledged and
edged with the let's-call-it-blessed light of day)
> between here and all northern waters—while
the lake's mirroring gleam beams back exactly
> her own flawless features and day and ducks and
dazzle-water are all at home for this here-and-now
> moment: afloat in this . . . their infinite affirmative.

acknowledgments

Thanks to the editors of the following magazines, in which versions of many of these poems first appeared—sometimes with different titles.

Agenda, Agni, Birmingham Poetry Review, Boston Review, Clifden Anthology, The Cortland Review, Cyphers, Gulf Coast, The Hampden-Sydney Poetry Review, The Irish Times, The Kenyon Review, The Literary Review, Little Star, The New Republic, The New Yorker, Poem-a-Day (Academy of American Poets), *Poetry Ireland Review, The Recorder, The Saint Ann's Review, Smartish Pace, The Stinging Fly, The Stony Thursday Book, Theodate, Tuba, The Warwick Review.*

"Owl Light" appeared in *Watching My Hands at Work: A Festschrift for Adrian Frazier,* edited by Eva Bourke, Megan Buckley, and Louis de Paor (Salmon Poetry, 2013).

"Leaving" and "The Cézanne Minute" (as "Minute") appeared in *Peter Fallon: Poet, Publisher, Editor and Translator,* edited by Richard Rankin Russell (Irish Academic Press, 2013).

And, as always, heartfelt thanks to Rachel.

Eamon Grennan was born in Dublin, Ireland, in 1941 and has spent over forty years living and working in the United States. An emeritus professor of English at Vassar College, he has also taught in the graduate creative writing programs at Columbia University and New York University. He is the author of numerous collections of poetry, published both in Ireland and the United States, including *Out of Sight: New & Selected Poems. Still Life with Waterfall* won the 2003 Lenore Marshall Poetry Prize of the Academy of American Poets. His collection of translations, *Leopardi: Selected Poems*, won the PEN Translation Award for Poetry. His translation (with Rachel Kitzinger) of *Oedipus at Colonus* was published by Oxford University Press in 2005. He has also published a book of criticism, *Facing the Music: Irish Poetry in the Twentieth Century*. He divides his time between Poughkeepsie, New York, and Renvyle, in the West of Ireland.

The text of *There Now* is set in Adobe Caslon Pro.
Book design by Rachel Holscher.
Composition by Bookmobile Design and Publishing Services,
Minneapolis, Minnesota.
Manufactured by Versa Press on acid-free,
30 percent postconsumer wastepaper.